Transparency in UK Company Supply Chains (Eradication of Slavery) Bill

CONTENTS

1. Disclosure by companies of measures to eradicate slavery, human trafficking, forced labour and the worst forms of child labour
2. Requirements of disclosure
3. Protections and rights for victims of slavery, human trafficking, forced labour and the worst forms of child labour
4. Short title, commencement and extent

A

BILL

TO

Require large companies in the UK to make annual statements of measures taken by them to eradicate slavery, human trafficking, forced labour and the worst forms of child labour (as set out in Article 3 of the International Labour Organisation's Convention No. 182) from their supply chains; to require such companies to provide customers and investors with information about measures taken by them to eliminate slavery, human trafficking, forced labour and the worst forms of child labour; to provide victims of slavery with necessary protections and rights; and for connected purposes.

B E IT ENACTED by the Queen's most Excellent Majesty, by and with the advice and consent of the Lords Spiritual and Temporal, and Commons, in this present Parliament assembled, and by the authority of the same, as follows:—

1 Disclosure by companies of measures to eradicate slavery, human trafficking, forced labour and the worst forms of child labour

(1) Every company operating in the United Kingdom and having annual worldwide gross receipts exceeding £100,000,000 shall disclose, as set forth in section 2, its efforts to eradicate slavery, human trafficking, forced labour and the worst forms of child labour from its direct supply chains for tangible goods and services offered for sale.

(2) In this Act "the worst forms of child labour" are those set out in Article 3 of the International Labour Organisation's Convention No. 182.

2 Requirements of disclosure

(1) The disclosure described in section 1 shall be—
 (a) set out in the company's annual report, and
 (b) posted on the company's internet website,
and a conspicuous and easily understood link to the required information shall be placed on the business homepage.

(2) If the company does not have an internet website, consumers shall be provided with the written disclosure within 30 days of the company receiving a written request for the disclosure from a consumer.

(3) The disclosure described in section 1 shall disclose to what extent, if any, the company does each of the following—

    (a) Engages in verification of product supply chains to evaluate and address risks of slavery, human trafficking, forced labour and the worst forms of child labour. The disclosure shall specify if the verification was not conducted by a person independent of the organisation being verified.

    (b) Conducts audits of suppliers to evaluate supplier compliance with company standards for slavery, human trafficking, forced labour and the worst forms of child labour in supply chains. The disclosure shall specify if the verification was not an independent, unannounced audit.

    (c) Requires direct suppliers to certify that materials incorporated into the product comply with the laws regarding slavery, human trafficking, forced labour and the worst forms of child labour of the country or countries in which they are doing business.

    (d) Maintains internal accountability standards, supply chain management and procurement systems, and procedures for employees or contractors failing to meet company's standards regarding slavery, human trafficking, forced labour and the worst forms of child labour. The disclosure shall describe such standards and systems.

    (e) Provides company employees and management who have direct responsibility for supply chain management with training on slavery, human trafficking, forced labour and the worst forms of child labour, with particular respect to mitigating risks within the supply chains of products.

    (f) Ensures that recruitment practices at all suppliers comply with the company's standards for eliminating exploitative labour practices that contribute to slavery, human trafficking, forced labour and the worst forms of child labour.

3 Protections and rights for victims of slavery, human trafficking, forced labour and the worst forms of child labour

Companies which uncover slavery, human trafficking, forced labour and the worst forms of child labour in their supply chains shall take action necessary and appropriate to assist people who have been victims and shall report on that action in their annual reports.

4 Short title, commencement and extent

(1) This Act may be cited as the Transparency in UK Company Supply Chains (Eradication of Slavery) Act 2012.

(2) This Act comes into force two months after Royal Assent.

(3) This Act extends to England and Wales, Northern Ireland and Scotland.

Transparency in UK Company Supply Chains (Eradication of Slavery) Bill

A

BILL

To require large companies in the UK to make annual statements of measures taken by them to eradicate slavery, human trafficking, forced labour and the worst forms of child labour (as set out in Article 3 of the International Labour Organisation's Convention No. 182) from their supply chains; to require such companies to provide customers and investors with information about measures taken by them to eliminate slavery, human trafficking, forced labour and the worst forms of child labour; to provide victims of slavery with necessary protections and rights; and for connected purposes.

Presented by Michael Connarty,
supported by
Tom Brake, Katy Clark,
Mr Tom Clarke, Ann Coffey,
Stella Creasy, Jim Dobbin,
Mark Durkan, Dr Julian Lewis,
Fiona Mactaggart, Jim Shannon
and Jim Sheridan.

Ordered, by The House of Commons,
to be Printed, 20 June 2012.

© Parliamentary copyright House of Commons 2012
This publication may be reproduced under the terms of the Parliamentary Click-Use Licence, available online through The National Archives website at
www.nationalarchives.gov.uk/information-management/our-services/parliamentary-licence-information.htm
Enquiries to The National Archives, Kew, Richmond, Surrey, TW9 4DU;
email: psi@nationalarchives.gsi.gov.uk

PUBLISHED BY AUTHORITY OF THE HOUSE OF COMMONS
LONDON — THE STATIONERY OFFICE LIMITED
Printed in the United Kingdom by The Stationery Office Limited
£1.50

ISBN 978-0-215-04214-9